Gold Stars

English

AGES 7-9 | KEY STAGE 2

PaRragon
Bath · New York · Cologne · Melbourne · Delhi
Hong Kong · Shenzhen · Singapore

This edition published by Parragon Books Ltd in 2018

Parragon Books Ltd
Chartist House
15–17 Trim Street
Bath BA1 1HA, UK
www.parragon.com

Copyright © Parragon Books Ltd 2009-2018

Written by Nina Filipek
Educational consultants: Martin Malcolm and Catherine Casey
Illustrated by Rob Davis/www.the-art-agency.co.uk
and Tom Connell/www.the-art-agency.co.uk

All rights reserved. No part of this publication may be reproduced, stored in a retrieval system or transmitted, in any form or by any means, electronic, mechanical, photocopying, recording or otherwise, without the prior permission of the copyright holder.

ISBN 978-1-5270-0240-1

Printed in China

Parents' page

The Gold Stars Key Stage 2 series

The Gold Stars Key Stage 2 series has been created to help your child practise key skills and information learned in school. Each book has been written by an expert team of teachers. This book will help your child to consolidate key skills in English, helping to develop confidence and understanding of the topics.

How to use this workbook

- Talk through the introductions to each topic and review the examples together.

- Encourage your child to tackle the fill-in activities independently.

- Keep work times short. Skip a page if it seems too difficult and return to it later.

- It doesn't matter if your child does some of the pages out of order.

- Answers to questions don't need to be complete sentences.

- Check the answers on pages 60-63. Encourage effort and reward achievement with praise.

- If your child finds any of the pages too difficult, don't worry. Children learn at different rates.

Contents

Spelling, grammar and punctuation

Spelling skills	6
Nouns and plurals	8
Prefixes and suffixes	10
Commas, questions, exclamations	12
Inverted commas	14
Apostrophes	16
Nouns, pronouns, connectives	18
Adjectives	20
Fronted adverbials	22
Tenses	24
Paragraphs	26
Clauses	28
Using a dictionary	30

Reading comprehension

Fiction

Fiction and non-fiction	32
Fables	34
Alliteration	36
Classic poetry	38
Playscripts	40

Non-fiction
Formal letters — 42
Instructions — 44
Information text — 46

Writing composition

Fiction
Shape and acrostic poems — 48
Characters — 50
Story plans and plots — 52

Non-fiction
Biography — 54
Persuasive writing — 56
Writing a review — 58

Answers — 60

Spelling skills

Learning objective: to learn different spelling methods

One way of learning to spell a new word is by using these 5 steps.
1. Look at the word
2. Say it
3. Cover it
4. Write it
5. Check it

Look for common letter patterns to spell these groups of words.

could, should, would

clown, frown, town

bridge, fudge, hedge

found, ground, loud, shout

coin, noise, soil, voice

cuddle, middle, little, table

A Sometimes you can find a root word or a word within a word.

Underline the root word in each of these groups of words.

cook	cooker	cookery
spark	sparkle	sparkler
clear	cleared	clearly
bedroom	bedstead	bedtime
sign	signal	signature

Do I have a tale or a tail?

B

Homophones are tricky words that sound the same but are spelled differently.

Write the correct homophone in each space below.

hear or here	ate or eight
right or write	beech or beach
would or wood	where, were or wear

DEFINITION

mnemonic: A picture or a clue to help you remember how to spell tricky words.

1. Teri is nearly ___eight___ years old.
2. I couldn't ___hear___ what she said.
3. I don't know if it's the ___right___ way.
4. ___Would___ you like to sleep over at my house?
5. ___Where___ can I get the bus into town?
6. We made sandcastles on the ___beach___.

List any other homophones that you know:

Pear or pair
bear or bare
Flour or flower
Sun or son

This is an example of a mnemonic; this **hear** has an **ear** in it!

Nouns and plurals

Learning objective: to learn plural forms of words

A noun is a person, a place or a thing. Nouns can be singular (only one) or plural (more than one).

A

When we make most words plural we add an **s** to the end. Write the plurals.

sausage**s**   cake**s**   drink__

book__   horse__   tree__

But if a word ends in **ch**, **sh**, **s**, **ss** or **x** we usually add **es**. Write the plurals.

dish**es**   kiss___   fox___   lunch___

bus___   wish___   cross___

If a noun ends in a consonant plus **y**, we drop the **y** and write **ies**. Write the plurals.

pony > **ponies**   baby > _____   story > _____

daisy > _____   cherry > _____   berry > _____

Some tricky plurals don't follow the rules. Learn them by heart.

| man > men | child > children | leaf > leaves |
| mouse > mice | goose > geese | person > people |

DEFINITION

vowels: a, e, i, o and u.
consonants: b, c, d, f, g, h, j, k, l, m, n, p, q, r, s, t, v, w, x, y, z.

B Read the poem below and turn the singular nouns into plurals. Mostly you can just add **s** but sometimes you have to rewrite the word in the space.

I Love the Seasons

I love it in the spring when the **bud__** burst into **million__** of tiny **flower__**.

I love it in the summer when we can make **sandcastle__** on the beach.

I love it in the autumn when the **leaf** _____ on the **tree__** turn from green to gold.

Best of all, I love it in the winter when we can make **snowman** _____.

The words **sheep**, **deer** and **fish** stay the same whether they are singular or plural.

C Change the nouns in bold in these sentences to plurals.

1. There is a **mouse** in the house! › There are _____ in the house!

2. There was only one **loaf**. › There were only two _____.

3. We saw a **goose** in the park. › We saw _____ in the park.

Prefixes and suffixes

Learning objective: to learn common prefixes and suffixes

Prefixes are extra letters added to the beginning of words. They change the meaning of the root word.

For example:

The rabbit appeared, then **dis**appeared, then **re**appeared!

A

Writing **un** at the beginning of these words will change their meaning. Try it and see!

untie ___fair
___lock ___do
___like ___lucky
___likely ___happy
___able ___hurt

Choose three words from the lists above to complete the dialogue below. Write the words in the spaces.

Tom's mum: I'm very _____ with you.

Tom: It's so _____ ! It wasn't my fault. I'm just _____ !

DEFINITION

prefixes: The extra letters added to the beginning of a word.
suffixes: The extra letters added to the end of a word.

B Underline words with prefixes in this passage. Look for **dis, re, im, un**.

Tom and Jez went to see a remake of Monsters of the Deep. Writing about it in a movie review for their school magazine, they said, "The monsters were unrealistic and unimaginative really. There was lots of action but the plot was disjointed and impossible to follow."

The word unsuccessful has a prefix *and* a suffix!

Suffixes are extra letters added to the end of words. Look at how they change the meaning of the root word.

For example:

hope > hopeless > hopeful   care > careful > careless

use > useful > useless   thought > thoughtful > thoughtless

C Choose a suffix to make sense of these sentences. Write **less** or **ful**.

1. It was very thought____ of Jenny to buy flowers.
2. The toy was use____ without a battery.
3. I felt hope____ at the start but then everything went wrong!
4. I knew I had to be care____ this time.

Commas, questions, exclamations

Learning objective: to learn basic punctuation

Commas tell readers to pause and take a moment to understand what a sentence is about.
- Put a comma after each item of a list.
- Never put a comma before the word 'and'.
- Put a comma after a group of words that belong together.

How to use commas:
- After each item in a list.
- To separate ideas within a sentence.

For example:

The huge plate was piled high with bacon, egg, mushrooms, fried onions, black pudding, baked beans and tomato!

A

Write the commas in these sentences.

1. We'll have two cornets with raspberry sauce a vanilla ice cream a carton of orange juice and a cup of tea please.

2. I'd like to order the tomato soup an egg and cress sandwich a banana smoothie and a chocolate muffin please.

3. The cat ran up the stairs down the corridor through the classroom and into Mrs Lane's office!

4. Go right at the lights turn right again at the T-junction then first left.

5. The children bought a ball a notebook a pencil case and some balloons.

> Sentences that ask questions usually begin with What, When, Where, Why or How.

Exclamation marks (!) show surprise or excitement.
Question marks (?) are used at the end of sentences when a question is asked.

B Read the sentences below and decide whether to write an exclamation mark or a question mark in each one.

1. Suddenly, all the lights went out __
2. "Aaaaaaaargh __" he cried.
3. Gina called out, "Hey, Tom __"
4. "What are 'gators __" she asked.
5. How do we know there's no life on Mars __

C Write 2 sentences with an exclamation mark at the end of each one.

D Write 2 sentences with a question mark at the end of each one.

Inverted commas

Learning objective: to learn how to use inverted commas

Inverted commas are drawn around the exact words that are spoken. This is called direct speech.

For example:
"How many children are coming?" asked Jason.

How to use inverted commas:
- Open the inverted commas at the start and close them at the end of the words spoken.
- All other punctuation goes inside the inverted commas.

A Write the missing inverted commas in the sentences below.

1. Tara cried, Wait for me!
2. Do you think he's an elf? asked Taylor.
3. Okay, said Sharon. What's wrong?
4. Wow! said Zac. You're a genius!

Inverted commas are sometimes called speech marks.

B Write the missing inverted commas in this story.

Ali and Bansi were in the Spooky Maize Maze.
 I think we must be lost, said Bansi, because I remember this path.
 A ghostly cry came from behind the hedge: Wooooh, wooooooh!
 Stop scaring me, said Ali.
 It's not me! replied Bansi.
 Help! they both cried.

Direct speech can come at either the beginning or the end of a sentence.

For example: "I'm only joking," Max said.   Max said, "I'm only joking."

Because the words complete the sentence a full stop is needed.

C Rewrite this sentence to put the direct speech at the end.

"These cakes are delicious," said the chef.

D Rewrite this sentence to put the direct speech at the beginning.

The vet said, "Dogs need a healthy diet."

Indirect (reported) speech does not need inverted commas.

For example:

Mira said that she would go. 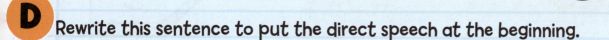 Mira said, "I will go."

Indirect speech → Direct speech

> Look at the way the pronouns (she/I) and verbs (would/will) change in the example.

E Use the example above to help you rewrite this indirect speech as direct speech.

1. Lauren said she felt ill.

2. Sam said it wasn't fair.

Apostrophes

Learning objective: to learn to use apostrophes

Apostrophes can shorten words or tell you to whom something belongs.

An apostrophe can replace missing letters:

For example:

do not ➜ don't   it is ➜ it's

we are ➜ we're   they will ➜ they'll

Apostrophes are tricky! Keep practising until you understand how they work.

A Shorten these words by using apostrophes.

1. cannot ➜ **can't**
2. should not ➜ _____
3. they will ➜ _____
4. she is ➜ _____
5. could not ➜ _____
6. we will ➜ _____
7. where is _____
8. they are ➜ _____

Apostrophes can also show possession.

For example: Ben's shoes.

B Rewrite each of these phrases using an apostrophe.

1. The shoes belonging to Ben   **Ben's shoes** _____
2. The book belonging to my friend _____
3. The lead belonging to the dog _____
4. The car belonging to Joe _____
5. The whiskers belonging to the cat _____

The possessive apostrophe can also tell you how many there are.

For example:
1. The boy's trainers were new. (one boy)
2. The boys' trainers were new. (more than one boy)

Remember these exceptions – the children's clothes, the men's clothes, the people's clothes.

If the noun is singular the apostrophe goes before the s.
If the noun is plural the apostrophe goes after the s.

C Rewrite each of these phrases using a possessive apostrophe.

1. The cat belonging to the girl.
   The girl's cat
2. The book belonging to the teacher.
3. The television belonging to the family.
4. The red nose belonging to the clown.
5. The pram belonging to the baby.
6. The house belonging to the dolls.
7. The drawings belonging to the children.
8. The race belonging to the men.

DEFINITION
To 'possess' means to 'own'.
possessive apostrophes: These are used to show who owns a particular thing.

Nouns, pronouns, connectives

Learning objective: to recognise nouns, pronouns, connectives

A noun is a naming word. It can be a person, place or thing.

For example:

The bee buzzed. **bee** is a noun.

Richard ran away. **Richard** is a noun.

The cats miaowed loudly. **cats** is a noun.

A Underline the nouns in these sentences:
1. The flowers were pretty.
2. I live in London.
3. The food was delicious.
4. Zak was asleep.
5. The girls laughed.
6. My sister has a laptop.

A pronoun is a word you can use to replace a noun so that you don't have to repeat it.

For example: Connor is kind. > He is kind.   **He** is a pronoun.

B Rewrite these sentences using pronouns. Choose from this list: him she it they them we

1. The flowers were pretty so I put the flowers in a vase.
   The flowers were pretty so I put them in a vase.
2. Zak was asleep and I didn't want to wake Zak up.
3. I like London because London has an interesting history.
4. The girls laughed because the girls thought it was funny.
5. Chris and I went swimming. Chris and I had a great time.

DEFINITION

Noun: A person, a place or a thing.
Pronoun: A word you can use instead of the noun.
Connective: A word that links ideas, sentences and paragraphs together.

Connectives are words that link ideas, sentences and paragraphs. Here are some useful connectives:

first, next, finally, consequently, later, suddenly, except, meanwhile, however, when, but, before, and, after, although, also, then

C Choose connectives from the list above to complete this school diary.

Taylor's school diary: Tuesday

<u>First</u>, we had a spelling test. _____ we wrote animal poems. _____ lunch, we had a visitor.
It was Mrs White. She'd brought her new baby to show us. _____ lunch, we had games outside on the field. _____, _____ it started to rain and we had to run inside. _____, it was our science lesson. _____, just before home time we had a story.

D Now write your diary for yesterday in the space below. Choose connectives to link your ideas and sentences together.

Yesterday, I woke up at...

Adjectives

Learning objective: to learn to use adjectives

Adjectives are used to describe people, places or things.

For example:

a **large** dog

a **small** dog

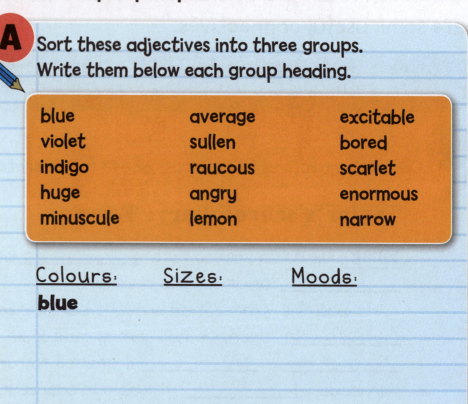

A Sort these adjectives into three groups. Write them below each group heading.

blue	average	excitable
violet	sullen	bored
indigo	raucous	scarlet
huge	angry	enormous
minuscule	lemon	narrow

Colours: Sizes: Moods:

blue

B Write a similar adjective (a synonym) for these common adjectives.

1. We had a nice time.
   We had a <u>great</u> time.
2. The pizza was okay.

3. The giant stomped his big foot.

4. It was a funny movie.

> This activity is the opposite of difficult. It's easy!

Opposite adjectives are known as antonyms.

C Write an antonym for each of these adjectives.

black › **white**
bold ›_____
hazy ›_____
hairy ›_____
unusual ›_____

scorching ›_____
expensive ›_____
popular ›_____
delicious ›_____
polite ›_____

D Change these adjectives to alter the meaning of the sentences.

1. A friendly, little dog came bounding up to her.
   A _____, _____ dog came bounding up to her.
2. It was an antique table.
   It was a _____ table.
3. It was a difficult job.
   It was an _____ job.
4. He was in a happy mood.
   He was in a _____ mood.
5. She went red when she saw him.
   She went _____ when she saw him.

DEFINITION
synonym: A word with a similar meaning.
antonym: A word with an opposite meaning.

Fronted adverbials

Learning objective: to know how to write a fronted adverbial

Fronted adverbials are used to emphasise when, where and how an action takes place. They are written at the front of the sentence.

How to use fronted adverbials:
- A comma is written after the fronted adverbial.
- An adverbial can be a single word, a phrase or a clause.

For example:
Look at how using fronted adverbials changes these sentences.
The fronted adverbials are underlined.

| They were tired at the end of the race. ↓ At the end of the race, they were tired. | The turtle slowly crawled out of the ocean. ↓ Slowly, the turtle crawled out of the ocean. | There were butterflies everywhere she looked. ↓ Everywhere she looked, there were butterflies. |

A Underline the fronted adverbials in these sentences.

1. In the end, they were happy.
2. Carefully, she crossed the stream.
3. Back at the house, there was no one home.
4. When the bell rang, they ran outside to play.

B Insert the missing commas after the fronted adverbials in these sentences.

1. In the morning it was sunny.
2. As it turned out they were lucky.
3. When the audience cheered they took a bow.
4. Later that day the storm broke.

C Draw lines to join these fronted adverbials to the correct endings.

1. On Saturday,   there was a tree house.
2. In the middle of the wood,   she went to Australia.
3. The following year,   the weekend begins.

D Rewrite the words in these sentences by moving the adverbials to the front. The first one has been done for you.

Don't forget to put capital letters, commas and full stops in the right places.

1. It went dark suddenly.
   Suddenly, it went dark.
2. She went to a friend's house after school.
3. The team lost every match before Marek joined them.
4. They sang 'Happy Birthday' when the candles were lit.

Tenses

Learning objective: to understand different tenses

The tense of the verbs in a sentence tells you when something happens.

The weather this week

Sat: sun
Sun: rain
Mon: snow
Tue: cloud
Wed: rain
Thurs: rain
Fri: sun

It rained last night.

It's snowing now!

It will be cloudy tomorrow.

A Today is Monday. Look at the weather chart above. Then write a sentence to answer each question.

1. What will the weather be like on Wednesday?

2. What was the weather like on Saturday?

3. What is the weather like today?

B Write the past, present or future tense sentences to complete the chart.

Past	Present	Future
It was hot.	It is hot.	_____
I was hot.	_____	_____
_____	He is hot.	He will be hot.
_____	We are hot.	_____
_____	_____	They will be hot.

To find out more about suffixes turn to page 10.

A suffix can change the time from the present to the past:

Present	Present continuous	Past	Present perfect
I play.	I am playing.	I played.	I have played.
I work.	I am working.	I worked.	I have worked.

C

Complete these present and past tense verbs.

Present	Present continuous	Past	Present perfect
I paint.	I am paint____.	I paint____.	I ____ painted.
I jump.	I am jump____.	I jump____.	I ____ jumped.
I shop.	I am shop____.	I shop____.	I ____ shopped.
I skip.	I am skip____.	I skip____.	I ____ skipped.

Irregular verbs don't follow the usual rules. Learn them by heart.

Present	Past
I get	I got
I have	I had
I go	I went

D

Change the verbs in this story from the present tense to the past tense.

I get out of the car and step in a puddle. We hear the band playing. They have started already! I run all the way to the hall.

I ____ out of the car and _____ in a puddle. We ____ the band playing. They ____ started already! I ____ all the way to the hall.

Paragraphs

Learning objective: to know how to write a paragraph

A paragraph is a piece of writing that focuses on one idea. It starts on a new line and sometimes has an indent or a number.

For example:

Sharks are my favourite animal. They have lived on Earth for over 400 million years. The most interesting thing about sharks is their teeth. They have thousands of them, set in rows, so when they lose a tooth another one moves forward to takes its place.

I wrote this paragraph about my favourite animal.

A Read the paragraph below, which talks about people's fear of sharks. Cross out the sentence that doesn't belong in this paragraph.

People are afraid of sharks but not all sharks are fierce. Many sharks are harmless to humans. The hammerhead shark has eyes on the sides of its head! In fact, more people die from bee stings than from shark attacks.

B Write a paragraph about your favourite animal. Try to write at least three sentences.

Your first sentence should tell the reader what the paragraph is about.

> To find out more about direct speech turn to page 14.

When you are writing direct speech, you start a new paragraph each time a new speaker starts.

For example:

"What would your superhero power be?" asked the teacher.
"I would like a super brain," Amir replied, "then I could solve all the world's problems."

C What superpowers do you think the other children in the class would like? Write what you think Flo and Jacob said in the gaps.

"What would your superhero power be?" the teacher asked Flo and Jacob.
"_____," Flo said, "_____."
"_____," said Jacob, "_____."

D The first part of each paragraph below is missing. Write the missing words. Choose from the following paragraph beginnings:

I would like x-ray vision
I would like to be able to change the weather

"_____," said Raj, "then we could have snowball fights in summer."
"_____," said Katja, "then I could find all the things I've lost in my bedroom."

Clauses

Learning objective: to know the difference between a main clause and a subordinate clause

A main clause is a group of words that makes sense by itself. A subordinate clause does not make sense by itself. It needs the main clause.

For example:

I love bones.
↑
Main clause

I love bones because I am a dog.
↑   ↑
Main clause   Subordinate clause

How to use subordinate clauses:
- A subordinate clause can go at the beginning of a sentence or later in a sentence.
- A subordinate clause begins with a conjunction (e.g. but, when, because, since, although, while, unless, after).

A Underline the subordinate clauses.

1. When I am older, I want to be an astronaut.
2. I must have grown, because these trousers are too short.
3. I'll meet you, after I've had lunch.
4. I said I was sorry, although it was an accident.

A subordinate clause is sometimes called a dependent clause.

B Underline the main clauses.

1. When I was six, I had a party.
2. I clean my teeth before I go to bed.
3. Unless it's raining, we're having a picnic.
4. While the cat's away, the mice will play!

Remember!
A main clause could make a sentence by itself.

I love chasing cats!
(That's a main clause.)

C

Write the missing conjunctions in the spaces. Choose from the list. Then underline the subordinate clauses.

while   unless   if   before

1. _____ you have a better idea, let's go to the cinema.
2. I would buy them, _____ you like them.
3. Stop, _____ going any further!
4. You can play in the garden, _____ I cook dinner.

D

Draw lines to join the main clauses and the subordinate clauses together.

Main clause	Subordinate clause
Run home	until it sets.
Put the jelly in the fridge	as it's your birthday.
I know it's time to get up	because my alarm clock is ringing.
You can go first	before it's too late!

DEFINITION
clause: A group of words that contains a verb and a noun or pronoun.

DEFINITION
conjunction: A type of connective that joins clauses within a sentence.

Using a dictionary

Learning objective: to know how to use a dictionary

A dictionary is a reference book that lists words and their meanings in alphabetical order.

For example:

doctor comes before **engineer**
scientist comes before **teacher**

d comes before **e**, and **s** comes before **t** in the alphabet.

The meaning of a word is called the definition.

A

For each list of words, write 1st, 2nd, 3rd or 4th in the boxes, according to the order they would appear in a dictionary.

Nouns

- lemur ☐
- tarantula ☐
- ostrich ☐
- armadillo ☐

Verbs

- knit ☐
- write ☐
- print ☐
- sew ☐

B

Draw lines to match the words to the correct definitions.

Word	Definition
dart	lean to one side
lurch	move uncomfortably
quake	move in circles
squirm	move quickly
twirl	shake with fright

> **DEFINITION**
> **alphabetical order:** When words are sorted according to the order in which their letters appear in the alphabet. If their first letters are the same, we look for the letters that come next.

C Read the words and the definitions. Write a sentence using each of the words defined.

1. **ideal**   something just right
   _____
   _____

2. **identical**   exactly the same
   _____
   _____

3. **imaginary**   not real
   _____
   _____

4. **immense**   very big
   _____
   _____

D Rewrite these two lists of words in alphabetical order. You may need to look at the second, third or fourth letters to sort them!

1. agree
   apple
   attach
   angle
   afraid
   asleep
   absent

2. quiz
   quiet
   quarter
   quell
   quack
   quest
   quick

31

Fiction and non-fiction

Learning objective: to distinguish between fiction and non-fiction

Fiction books contain made-up stories. Non-fiction books contain information and fact. Fiction and non-fiction books are written in different ways.

Fiction books usually have:
- dialogue
- characters
- a story or plot
- illustrations

Non-fiction books usually have:
- information and facts
- photographs
- diagrams or maps
- an index

A

Label these book titles as either F for fiction or NF for non-fiction. Write in the box next to each one.

1. How Volcanoes Work ☐
2. Primary Science ☐
3. Bedtime Stories ☐
4. Teddy Goes to Toytown ☐
5. A History of the Vikings ☐
6. Treasure Island ☐

DEFINITION

dialogue: Conversation and words that are spoken.

index: An alphabetical list of things in a book, with the page numbers on which each one appears, to make it easy to find things.

My book is called *Morris and the Aliens*. Do you think it is fiction or non-fiction?

Sort your books at home into fiction and non-fiction collections.

B Read the texts A, B and C extracted from different books and match them to the correct book titles below:

Disappearing Worlds   Wizardy Woo   Secrets and Spies

A. It was on the night of the next full moon that things began to go wrong. Spells that had worked perfectly well for hundreds of years had suddenly lost their magic....

From title: _____

B. Supergirl sped past the secret agents in her souped-up spy car. She had to reach Point Blank before they did. Her secret life depended on it!

From title: _____

C. The world's rainforests are vitally important to us. But every hour, thousands of square kilometres of trees are being cut down all over the world.

From title: _____

C Which of these books would be in the fiction section and which in the non-fiction section of a library? Write the titles in the correct columns.

Fiction   Non-fiction

Fables

Learning objective: to learn to predict text in sentences

A fable is a short story with a moral lesson. The characters in fables are often animals.

A In Aesop's fable of 'The Dog and His Bone' below, some words have been left out. Predict what the words might be and write them in the spaces.

A dog was hurrying home with a big bone _____ the butcher had given him. He growled at everyone _____ passed, worried that they might try to steal it _____ him. He planned to bury the bone in the _____ and eat it later.

As he crossed a bridge _____ a stream, the dog happened to look down into _____ water. There he saw another dog with a much _____ bone. He didn't realise he was looking at his _____ reflection! He growled at the other dog and it _____ back.

The greedy dog wanted that bone too, and _____ snapped at the dog in the water. But then _____ own big bone fell into the stream with a _____ , and quickly sank out of sight. Then he realised _____ foolish he had been.

Who was Aesop?

Aesop was probably a Greek storyteller who lived over 2000 years ago.

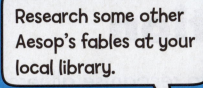

Research some other Aesop's fables at your local library.

B

Write sentences to answer these questions about 'The Dog and His Bone'.

1. Why was the dog hurrying home?

2. Why did the other dog growl back?

3. What lesson do you think the dog learned?

4. What is the moral of the fable? Tick the correct answer: a, b or c.
   a) Waste not want not.
   b) It is foolish to be greedy.
   c) Be happy with how you look.

5. If you rewrote the fable using the same moral but a different animal character, which animal would you choose? Say why.

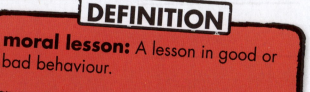

DEFINITION
moral lesson: A lesson in good or bad behaviour.

Alliteration

Learning objective: to recognise alliteration

Alliteration is when we put together words that start with the same sound.

For example: This monster movie is a massive hit.

Write each idea on a new line.

A Write a list poem, using alliteration.

One wiggly worm.

Two _____ _____

Three _____ _____

Four _____ _____

Five _____ _____

Six _____ _____

Seven _____ _____

Eight _____ _____

Nine _____ _____

Ten _____ _____

I'm jumping for joy! Is that an alliteration?

B Complete the magazine headlines below using alliteration. Choose words from this list.

| DOGS | LONG | TWOSOME | LOCKS | TERRIBLE | RECYCLE | DRAMA |

REUSE AND _____

DANCING _____ **IN SCHOOL** _____

TWINS ARE A _____ _____

LOOK AFTER YOUR _____ _____

C Complete these sentences using fun alliterations.

My alligator   is called Albert   and he's adorable.
My bear   is called Baloo   and he's big.
My c_____   is called C_____   and he's c_____.
My d_____   is called D_____   and she's d_____.
My e_____   is called E_____   and she's e_____.
My f_____   is called F_____   and she's f_____.

DEFINITION

alliteration: Words that begin with the same sounds.

Classic poetry

Learning objective: to understand different types of poems

Read this extract from 'The Pied Piper of Hamelin' by Robert Browning.

Rats!
They fought the dogs, and killed the cats,
And bit the babies in the cradles,
And ate the cheeses out of the vats,
And licked the soup from the cook's own ladles,
Split open the kegs of salted sprats,
Made nests inside men's Sunday hats,
And even spoiled the women's chats,
By drowning their speaking
With shrieking and squeaking
In fifty different sharps and flats.

A

Now answer the questions.

1. What is the extract about?

2. Look at the first two lines. Which words are alliterations – that is, begin with the same sounds?

3. Find five words in the poem that rhyme with **cats**.

> **DEFINITION**
> **classic:** A classic is a great book or piece of writing usually from long ago.

Robert Browning was a famous writer who lived from 1812 to 1889.

4. What is a **ladle**?

5. How many cooks are there? What does the apostrophe in **cook's** tell us?

6. Why do you think the poet chose these three words: **speaking, shrieking** and **squeaking**?

7. What are **Sunday hats**?

8. Which two lines of the poem show that the rats make a tuneless and annoying noise?

9. If you've heard the story of the Pied Piper of Hamelin, write down what you know about it. If you're not familiar with the story, try to find a library copy.

DEFINITION

cradle: A small cot that swings.
sprat: A small fish.

Playscripts

Learning objective: to understand how to read a playscript

Read the playscript below.

Scene 1: A New Puppy
Two dogs talking in the park.
Characters:
   Buster: Bulldog
   Sindy: Yorkshire Terrier

BUSTER: (wailing) A new puppy! After everything I've done for them.

SINDY: I knew you'd be upset. I told Mindy when I heard.

BUSTER: I take them for lovely walks, I eat up all their leftovers – even that takeaway muck they always dish out on a Friday… and this is the thanks I get!

SINDY: (sympathetically) You can choose your friends but you can't choose your owners.

BUSTER: What can they want a puppy for anyway?

SINDY: Well, puppies are cute.

BUSTER: Cute! Aren't I cute enough for them?

SINDY: Er…

BUSTER: Well, I'm telling you now. It's not getting its paws on my toys. I've buried them all!

How to write a playscript:
- Write the speaker's name then what they say.
- Start a new line for each speaker.

How to write a prose story:
- Start a new paragraph for each speaker.
- Put speech marks around the words spoken and include the speaker's name in the sentence.

DEFINITION

playscript: The text of a play, including a list of characters, what the actors say and their actions on stage.

A Now rewrite the playscript as a prose story. Fill in the missing words.

Chapter 1: A New Puppy

"_____!" Buster wailed. "_____
_____."

"I knew you'd be upset," replied Sindy. "_____."

"I take them for lovely walks, I eat up all their leftovers – even that takeaway muck they always dish out on a Friday _____
_____!" said Buster.

"You can choose your friends but you can't choose your owners," _____.

"_____?" cried Buster.

"Well, puppies are cute," said Sindy.

"_____?" replied Buster.

"Er..." said Sindy.

"Well, I'm telling you now," said Buster. "_____
_____!"

Formal letters

Learning objective: to read and understand a formal letter

Read these formal letters and write a sentence to answer each question.

> 6 Acorn Avenue,
> Newbridge,
> N16 5BH
>
> Monday, 7 May 2017
>
> Dear Miss Smith,
>
> I would be grateful if you would allow Becky to leave school early tomorrow afternoon. She has an appointment at the dentist at 3.15 pm but I need to pick her up from school at 2.45 pm. I'm sorry that she will miss the last lesson of the day but this was the only time available.
>
> As Tuesday is homework night, perhaps I could take Becky's homework with me when I come to collect her.
>
> Yours sincerely,
>
> Mrs Alice Kenwood

A

1. If Becky's appointment is at 3.15 pm why does she need to leave at 2.45 pm?

2. On what day of the week is Becky's appointment?

3. Why does Mrs Kenwood apologise for taking Becky early?

4. Becky thinks she won't have to do her homework. Is this true?

DEFINITION

formal letter: A business letter to someone who is not a personal friend.

Mrs A Kenwood,
6 Acorn Avenue,
Newbridge,
N16 5BH

Monday, 7 May 2017

Botchit Kitchens,
Dead End Lane,
Newbridge,
NO1 1NR

Dear Sir,

I am writing to complain about your company's shoddy workmanship on my recently fitted new kitchen.

Firstly, all of the doors are hanging off their hinges. Secondly, the drawers have been fitted upside-down so we can't put anything in them. Thirdly, you forgot to make room for the sink! What use is a kitchen without a sink?

I want to know when you are able to put these things right. Please call me to arrange a time as soon as possible.

Yours faithfully,

Mrs A Kenwood

B

1. Whose address is printed on the left-hand side of the page?

2. What does 'shoddy' mean in the first sentence?

3. What is the purpose of the letter?

4. From reading the letter, how do you think Mrs Kenwood is feeling?

Instructions

Learning objective: to understand instruction text

Read the instructions and then answer the questions below.

Apple and Raspberry Refresher

Ingredients (serves 1):
4 ice cubes
1 tablespoon raspberry syrup
250 ml apple juice
thin slices of apple for decoration

What you do:
1. Put the ice cubes in a plastic bag and crush them with a rolling pin.
2. Tip the ice into a glass.
3. Pour on the raspberry syrup.
4. Fill the glass to the top with apple juice.
5. Decorate with thin slices of apple.

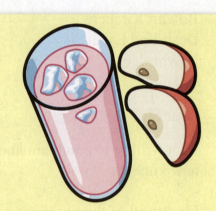

A

1. What other things will you need in addition to the list of ingredients?

2. Is there enough for two glasses?

3. Do you need apple slices to make this drink?

4. The instructions include the following words: put, tip, pour, fill, decorate. Are these words nouns, verbs or adjectives?

5. Write an alternative name for this drink.

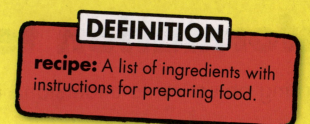

DEFINITION

recipe: A list of ingredients with instructions for preparing food.

Look at the recipe and read the instructions. Can you spot any missing ingredients?

Chicken Salad Supreme Sandwich

Ingredients:
bread
margarine
cooked chicken
lettuce leaves
tomatoes

What you do:
1. Butter the bread.
2. Put the chicken on the bread.
3. Spread on some mayonnaise.
4. Add tomatoes and lettuce.
5. Then sandwich together.

This recipe is badly written because:
- The list of ingredients is incomplete.
- We don't know how much we need of anything.
- Some steps are missing from **What you do**.

B Rewrite the recipe in your own words. Try to make big improvements on the original.

45

Information text

Learning objective: to understand information text

Read this page carefully, then write a sentence to answer each question about it on the opposite page.

The Spanish Armada

In 1587, Elizabeth I was Queen of England and Philip II was King of Spain. The two leaders disagreed over religion. When Elizabeth signed a death warrant for the Catholic Mary Queen of Scots to be executed, it was the final straw for Philip. He ordered an invasion.

In 1588, Philip sent an Armada of 130 warships to invade England. But the English saw them coming and set sail, meeting the Spanish Armada in the English Channel. The Spanish ships sailed in a crescent shape around the English fleet. The English knew they would have to break this formation to defeat the Armada.

So the English sent burning ships to sail into the Spanish Armada. The plan worked and the Armada scattered. The Spanish ships were large, heavy and slow to move and turn. The English ships were smaller and could turn quickly. They had better cannons too, which caused a lot of damage to the Spanish ships.

The Armada tried to escape back to Spain by sailing north but bad weather blew the ships towards the coasts of Ireland and Scotland. Many ships were wrecked against the rocks.

Only half of the ships that set out in the Armada made it back to Spain. None of the English ships was lost. It was one of Elizabeth's greatest victories.

DEFINITION

crescent: A curved shape.
death warrant: An order to put somebody to death.
Catholic: A member of the Roman Catholic Church.

Information text is found in non-fiction books.

A

1. Why do you think Philip was angry when Mary Queen of Scots was executed?

2. What does 'it was the final straw for Philip' mean?

3. Why would a crescent shape of Spanish ships be a problem for the English?

4. How did the English plan to break up the Armada?

5. What advantages did the English ships have?

6. Where was the Armada shipwrecked?

7. Approximately how many Spanish ships survived the battle?

8. How many English ships survived?

Shape and acrostic poems

Learning objective: to write a shape poem and an acrostic poem

Read the shape poem.

Egg
Yellow yolk for my breakfast, with dip-in soldiers. I love eggy bread, boiled, fried, scrambled, or poached eggs... How do you like your eggs? "Made from chocolate, of course!"

How to write a **shape poem**:
- Draw an outline of a familiar object.
- Write your poem inside the outline, following the shape.
- Don't worry about rhyme - it doesn't have to rhyme.
- Try to include alliteration, e.g. yellow yolk.

A This circle shape could represent a ball, a bubble, the Sun or the Moon - you decide. Then write a shape poem of your own inside the circle.

DEFINITION

acrostic: A poem or other piece of text in which some of the letters spell out a word when you read downwards.

This is an acrostic poem. The first letter in each line spells a name.

My brother
Always kicking a ball or
Running recklessly
CRASH! Into me!
OUCH! Look where you're going!

Here's another example:

PLAYFUL
C**U**TE
YEL**P**
PAW
FURR**Y**

How to write an **acrostic poem**:
- Write about something or someone that you know well.
- Spell out the subject of your poem vertically down the page.
- Alongside each letter continue with a descriptive phrase or word.

B Write an acrostic poem of your own in the space below.

49

Characters

Learning objective: to write a character description

Read the character descriptions and answer the questions below.

1. Grandpa Bob, old and gnarled, like an ancient oak, sits rooted in his armchair, surrounded by his books. Age has not dulled his sense of humour or his mind, which is still as sharp and clear as ever.

2. Auntie Deera was round and plump with a soft, sunny face. When she laughed, which was often, her tummy laughed too. Her favourite saying was, "You'll never guess what happened to me today…"

3. Zak was a terrible two-year-old and a tearaway at ten. Every day at primary school, his cheeky grin got him into and out of mischief. "It wasn't me!" he'd say.

4. Charlie's blue eyes are outlined with thick, black mascara. A skull tattoo on her arm makes her look hard, but I know she's not.

A

1. Which of the characters is more likely to read books: Auntie Deera or Grandpa Bob?

2. Which of the characters is most likely to enjoy food? Say why.

3. Rewrite the description of Auntie Deera using opposite adjectives to change her character.
   Auntie Deera was _____ and _____ with a _____, _____ face.

4. Which of the characters is the youngest? Say why.

5. How old do you think Charlie is?

Try writing a description of me! What adjectives would you use?

B Write descriptions for each of these characters. Describe their personalities and behaviour, as well as what they look like.

Miss Harshly, teacher

Bulky Bazza, weightlifter

A.T., alien being

Write a character description of someone that you know well. Disguise their true identity by changing their name, as many writers do!

How to write a character description:
- Choose names carefully that suggest a character, e.g. Mrs Jolly.
- Ask yourself questions, e.g. What's their personality? What do they like to do?
- Different characters should speak differently, e.g. they might have favourite sayings.
- Give your character an unusual feature, e.g. eyes of different colours.

Story plans and plots

Learning objective: to learn how to plan a story

Now it's time to write your own story. Try these story-planning tips.

1. Choose a book you have enjoyed and imitate it, changing the setting, the characters and the events.

   > **For example:** you could write a story based on 'The Three Billy Goats Gruff' but change the troll to a bully and the Billy Goats Gruff to you and your friends!
   >
   > I was walking home from school with Gaz and Tim when we saw him, swinging on the gate.

2. Retell something that has happened to you but change the characters and the setting.

   > **For example:** write a story based on something you lost. Perhaps it belonged to someone else!
   >
   > Where could it have gone? I'm in big trouble now. Mum doesn't even know I had it!

3. Use more than one theme, e.g. good and evil, friendship, lost and found, a long journey, rags to riches.

   > **For example:** write a story that explores two themes – friendship and rags to riches.
   >
   > Cindy carried her empty suitcase to the station. She pretended it was heavy so that the others wouldn't know she had nothing to put in it.

The characters should be changed by the events in your story. For example, an evil character might see the error of his or her ways and become a good person.

Don't try to write your story without first making a plan. Your plan might be a spider diagram, a storyboard or a written list. Look at these plans for a retelling of 'The Three Billy Goats Gruff'.

The Troll and the Three Billy Goats (retold)

Storyboard

| Billy goats teasing troll | Troll lonely | Small billy goat falls |
| Troll saves him | Making friends | Troll is happy |

List

1. Billy Goats tease Troll.
2. Troll is lonely.
3. Smallest Billy Goat falls off the bridge.
4. Troll saves him.
5. Billy Goats make friends with Troll.
6. Now Troll is happy.

Spider diagram

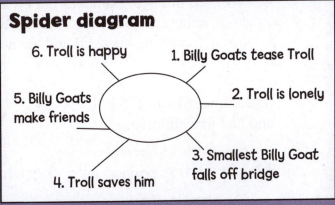

1. Billy Goats tease Troll
2. Troll is lonely
3. Smallest Billy Goat falls off bridge
4. Troll saves him
5. Billy Goats make friends
6. Troll is happy

Now try planning and writing your own story on a separate piece of paper.

53

Biography

Learning objective: to understand how to write a biography

A book or a piece of writing that is an account of a person's life is called a biography.

A The paragraphs below are all from the biography of Roald Dahl. But they are mixed up. Read them carefully and then write the order you think they go in.

Biography of Roald Dahl (1916–1990)

1. After school, he worked for the Shell Petroleum Company in Tanzania and in 1939, at the start of the Second World War, he joined the Royal Air Force.

2. He recovered and resumed duties in 1941 but then he started to suffer from headaches and blackouts.

3. Sadly, when he was just four, his seven-year-old sister died from appendicitis and a month later his father died from pneumonia.

4. He began writing in 1942 after being sent home from the army. His most popular children's books include *Charlie and the Chocolate Factory*, *James and the Giant Peach* and *The BFG*.

5. In 1940, Dahl was out on a mission when he was forced to make an emergency landing. Unluckily he hit a boulder and his plane crashed, fracturing his skull and his nose and temporarily blinding him.

6. Dahl married in 1953 and had five children.

7. Roald Dahl was born in Cardiff in 1916, the son of Norwegian parents.

I think that the paragraphs should go in the following order:

DEFINITION

timeline: A line representing a period of time on which dates and events are marked.

B Write a biography of a friend or relative. Use this space to plan a timeline of their life, writing key events above the line and dates below it.

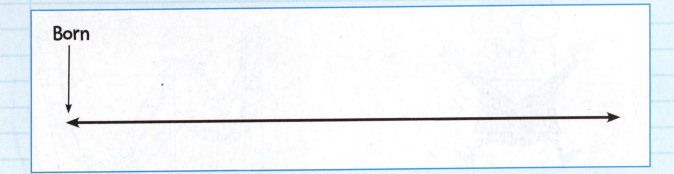

Now write the biography in this space.

55

Persuasive writing

Learning objective: to learn to write persuasively

Read the snippets of text taken from an advertising leaflet for Awesome Towers.

AWESOME TOWERS!

- Have you got what it takes to ride the biggest rollercoaster?
- Special holiday season tickets
- Park and ride
- Gift shop
- New this year!

AWESOME TOWERS!

- A fabulous day out for all the family!
- There's something for everyone...
- Fantastic fun-packed activities for all ages.
- Ride awesome rollercoasters.
- Watch spectacular live shows.
- Enjoy an excellent choice of cafés and restaurants.
- You're guaranteed to have fun!

"Next time you visit an attraction pick up a leaflet and notice how it is written."

A Now write a leaflet advertising a major attraction near you.

Amazing day out! Come rain or shine!

Holiday discount prices
Buy one ticket, get one free!

How to write persuasive text:
- Use adjectives, e.g. biggest, best, terrific, exciting, guaranteed, great.
- Use verbs, e.g. enjoy, see, find, discover, watch, ride, go, eat.
- Speak to the reader, e.g. use the pronoun 'you'.

Writing a review

Learning objective: to write a review of a book, song or film

Read the book review below. Notice how it is set out under different headings.

<u>Title</u>: Kensuke's Kingdom
<u>Author</u>: Michael Morpurgo

<u>Brief outline of the story</u>
The story is about a boy called Michael and his family who set off to sail around the world. One stormy night, Michael and his dog get washed overboard. They are rescued by Kensuke, an old man who lives on a desert island.

<u>Strengths</u>
I liked the way the author wrote about the friendship between Michael and Kensuke. It seemed very real, like a true story.

<u>Weaknesses</u>
I think it was sad at the end when Michael left the island. I usually prefer stories with happier endings. But if Michael had stayed, his parents would have been unhappy.

<u>Recommendation</u>
This is a wonderful book. Children over 8 years old would enjoy it, as I have.

<u>Score</u>
9/10

DEFINITION
review: An opinion or criticism of something.

Write a list of your top three books, songs and films.

A

Write a review of a book, song or film that you have enjoyed.

Title:
Author/artist:
Brief outline of the story/song

Strengths

Weaknesses

Recommendation

Score
    /10

How to write a review:
- Give details about the book/song/film.
- Write about the things you liked.
- Write about the things you didn't like.
- Give a recommendation: say who would enjoy it.

Answers

Page 6

A spark, sparkle, sparkler
   clear, cleared, clearly
   bedroom, bedstead, bedtime
   sign, signal, signature

Page 7

B 1. eight 2. hear 3. right 4. Would 5. Where
   6. beach

Page 8

A sausages, cakes, drinks, books, horses, trees
   dishes, kisses, foxes, lunches, buses, wishes, crosses
   ponies, babies, stories, daisies, cherries, berries

Page 9

B buds, millions, flowers, sandcastles, leaves, trees, snowmen

C 1. There are mice in the house! 2. There were only two loaves. 3. We saw geese in the park.

Page 10

A untie, unlock, unlike, unlikely, unable, unfair, undo, unlucky, unhappy, unhurt

   I'm very unhappy with you. / It's so unfair! / I'm just unlucky!

Page 11

B Tom and Jez went to see a remake of Monsters of the Deep. Writing about it in a movie review for their school magazine, they said, "The monsters were unrealistic and unimaginative really. There was lots of action but the plot was disjointed and impossible to follow."

C 1. thoughtful 2. useless 3. hopeful 4. careful

Page 12

A 1. We'll have two cornets with raspberry sauce, a vanilla ice cream, a carton of orange juice and a cup of tea, please.
   2. I'd like to order the tomato soup, an egg and cress sandwich, a banana smoothie and a chocolate muffin, please.
   3. The cat ran up the stairs, down the corridor, through the classroom and into Mrs Lane's office!
   4. Go right at the lights, turn right again at the T-junction, then first left.
   5. The children bought a ball, a notebook, a pencil case and some balloons.

Page 13

B 1. Suddenly, all the lights went out!
   2. "Aaaaaaaargh!" he cried.
   3. Gina called out, "Hey, Tom!"
   4. "What are 'gators?" she asked.
   5. How do we know there's no life on Mars?

Page 14

A 1. Tara cried, "Wait for me!"
   2. "Do you think he's an elf?" asked Taylor.
   3. "Okay," said Sharon. "What's wrong?"
   4. "Wow!" said Zac. "You're a genius!"

B Ali and Bansi were in the Spooky Maize Maze.
   "I think we must be lost," said Bansi, "because I remember this path."
   A ghostly cry came from behind the hedge: "Wooooh, wooooooh!"
   "Stop scaring me," said Ali.
   "It's not me!" replied Bansi.
   "Help!" they both cried.

Page 15

C The chef said, "These cakes are delicious."
D "Dogs need a healthy diet," said the vet.
E 1. Lauren said, "I feel ill."
   2. Sam said, "It isn't fair."

Page 16

A 1. can't 2. shouldn't 3. they'll 4. she's 5. couldn't
   6. we'll 7. where's 8. they're
B 1. Ben's shoes 2. My friend's book 3. The dog's lead
   4. Joe's car 5. The cat's whiskers

Page 17

C 1. The girl's cat 2. The teacher's book
   3. The family's television 4. The clown's red nose
   5. The baby's pram 6. The dolls' house
   7. The children's drawings
   8. The men's race

Page 18

A 1. The flowers were pretty.
   2. I live in London.
   3. The food was delicious.
   4. Zak was asleep.
   5. The girls laughed.
   6. My sister has a laptop.

Page 18 continued

B 1. The flowers were pretty so I put <u>them</u> in a vase.
2. Zak was asleep and I didn't want to wake <u>him</u> up.
3. I like London because <u>it</u> has an interesting history.
4. The girls laughed because <u>they</u> thought it was funny.
5. Chris and I went swimming. <u>We</u> had a great time.

Page 19

C Possible answers:
<u>First</u>, we had a spelling test. <u>Then</u> we wrote animal poems. <u>Before</u> lunch, we had a visitor. It was Mrs White. She'd brought her new baby to show us. <u>After</u> lunch, we had games outside on the field. <u>However</u>, <u>suddenly</u> it started to rain and we had to run inside. <u>Next</u>, it was our science lesson. <u>Finally</u>, just before home time we had a story.

Page 20

A Colours: blue, lemon, scarlet, violet, indigo.
Sizes: huge, enormous, minuscule, average, narrow.
Moods: sullen, raucous, excitable, angry, bored.

B Possible answers:
1. We had a <u>great</u> time.
2. The pizza was <u>average</u>.
3. The giant stomped his <u>huge</u> foot.
4. It was an <u>hilarious</u> movie.

Page 21

C black > white   scorching > freezing
bold > shy   expensive > cheap
hazy > clear   popular > unpopular
hairy > bald (or hairless)   delicious > horrible (or disgusting)
unusual > common (or normal)   polite > rude

D Possible answers:
1. A <u>fierce</u>, <u>big</u> dog came bounding up to her.
2. It was a <u>new</u> table.
3. It was an <u>easy</u> job.
4. He was in a <u>sad</u> mood.
5. She went <u>white</u> when she saw him.

Page 22

1. <u>In the end</u>, they were happy.
2. <u>Carefully</u>, she crossed the stream.
3. <u>Back at the house</u>, there was no one home.
4. <u>When the bell rang</u>, they ran outside to play.

Page 23

B 1. In the morning, it was sunny.
2. As it turned out, they were lucky.
3. When the audience cheered, they took a bow.
4. Later that day, the storm broke.

C 1. On Saturday, the weekend begins.
2. In the middle of the wood, there was a tree house.
3. The following year, she went to Australia.

D 1. Suddenly, it went dark.
2. After school, she went to a friend's house.
3. Before Marek joined them, the team lost every match.
4. When the candles were lit, they sang 'Happy Birthday'.

Page 24

A 1. It will rain on Wednesday. 2. It was sunny on Saturday.
3. It is snowing today.

B

Past	Present	Future
It was hot.	It is hot.	<u>It will be hot.</u>
I was hot.	<u>I am hot.</u>	<u>I will be hot.</u>
<u>He was hot.</u>	He is hot.	<u>He will be hot.</u>
<u>We were hot.</u>	We are hot.	<u>We will be hot.</u>
<u>They were hot.</u>	<u>They are hot.</u>	They will be hot.

Page 25

C I am painting. I painted. I have painted.
I am jumping. I jumped. I have jumped.
I am shopping. I shopped. I have shopped.
I am skipping. I skipped. I have skipped.

D I <u>got</u> out of the car and <u>stepped</u> in a puddle.
We <u>heard</u> the band playing. They <u>had</u> started already!
I <u>ran</u> all the way to the hall.

Page 26

A The sentence that does not belong: The hammerhead shark has eyes on the sides of its head!

Page 27

D "I would like to be able to change the weather," said Raj, "then we could have snowball fights in summer."
"I would like x-ray vision," said Katja, "then I could find all the things I've lost in my bedroom."

Page 28

A 1. <u>When I am older</u>, I want to be an astronaut.
2. I must have grown, <u>because these trousers are too short</u>.
3. I'll meet you, <u>after I've had lunch</u>.
4. I said I was sorry, <u>although it was an accident</u>.

61

Answers

Page 28 continued

B When I was six, I had a party.
I clean my teeth before I go to bed.
Unless it's raining, we're having a picnic.
While the cat's away, the mice will play!

Page 29

C Unless you have a better idea, let's go to the cinema.
I would buy them, if you like them.
Stop, before going any further!
You can play in the garden, while I cook dinner.

D Run home → before it's too late!
Put the jelly in the fridge → until it sets.
I know it's time to get up → because my alarm clock is ringing.
You can go first → as it's your birthday.

Page 30

A Nouns: 1st armadillo, 2nd lemur, 3rd ostrich, 4th tarantula
Verbs: 1st knit, 2nd print, 3rd sew, 4th write

B dart → move quickly
lurch → lean to one side
quake → shake with fright
squirm → move uncomfortably
twirl → move in circles

Page 31

D 1. absent, afraid, agree, angle, apple, asleep, attach
2. quack, quarter, quell, quest, quick, quiet, quiz

Page 32

A 1. How Volcanoes Work – NF
2. Primary Science – NF
3. Bedtime Stories – F
4. Teddy Goes to Toytown – F
5. A History of the Vikings – NF
6. Treasure Island – F

Challenge: Morris and the Aliens is fiction.

Page 33

B A. Wizardy Woo   B. Secrets and Spies
C. Disappearing Worlds

C Fiction: Wizardy Woo, Secrets and Spies
Non-fiction: Disappearing Worlds

Page 34

A Possible answers:
A dog was hurrying home with a big bone that the butcher had given him. He growled at everyone who/he passed, worried that they might try to steal it from him. He planned to bury the bone in the garden and eat it later.
As he crossed a bridge over a stream, the dog happened to look down into the water. There he saw another dog with a much bigger bone. He didn't realise he was looking at his own reflection! He growled at the other dog and it growled back.
The greedy dog wanted that bone too, and he snapped at the dog in the water. But then his own big bone fell into the stream with a splash, and quickly sank out of sight. Then he realised how foolish he had been.

Page 35

B 1. He was hurrying to get home quickly before someone stole the bone from him.
2. The other dog growled back because it was just a reflection.
3. The dog learned that he had lost his bone because he was greedy.
4. b) It is foolish to be greedy.

Page 37

B REUSE AND RECYCLE   DANCING DOGS IN SCHOOL DRAMA
TWINS ARE A TERRIBLE TWOSOME   LOOK AFTER YOUR LONG LOCKS

Pages 38–39

A 1. The extract tells us about the rats.
2. killed/cats/cradles; bit/babies
3. vats, sprats, hats, chats, flats
4. A ladle is a big spoon.
5. The apostrophe tells us that there is only one cook.
6. They all begin with an 's' sound. They also rhyme.
7. They are worn on Sunday when going to church.
8. 'With shrieking and squeaking
In fifty different sharps and flats.'

Page 41

A "A new puppy!" Buster wailed. "After everything I've done for them."

"I knew you'd be upset," replied Sindy. "I told Mindy when I heard."

"I take them for lovely walks, I eat up all their leftovers – even that takeaway muck they always dish out on a Friday... and this is the thanks I get!" said Buster.

"You can choose your friends but you can't choose your owners," said Sindy, sympathetically.

"What can they want a puppy for anyway?" cried Buster.

"Well, puppies are cute," said Sindy.

"Cute! Aren't I cute enough for them?" replied Buster.

"Er ..." said Sindy.

"Well, I'm telling you now," said Buster. "It's not getting its paws on my toys. I've buried them all!"

Page 42

A 1. She needs to leave at 2.45 pm in order to get to the appointment on time.
2. Becky's appointment is on Tuesday.
3. Mrs Kenwood apologises because Becky will miss a lesson.
4. Becky will have to do her homework because Mrs Kenwood is going to collect it.

Page 43

B 1. The kitchen company's address is on the left.
2. Shoddy means careless and of poor quality.
3. Mrs Kenwood wants the company to put right these mistakes.
4. She is exasperated, disappointed and annoyed.

Page 44

A 1. You need a plastic bag, rolling pin and glass.
2. No there isn't enough for two glasses because the ingredients list states 'serves 1'.
3. No, because the apple slices are for decoration only.
4. These words are verbs.

Page 47

A 1. Philip was angry because she was a Catholic and he was too.
2. 'It was the final straw' means that Philip will take some action.
3. The English ships could then be attacked on three sides.
4. The plan was to sail burning ships into them.
5. The English ships were smaller, faster and had better cannons.
6. The Armada was shipwrecked off the coasts of Ireland and Scotland.
7. About 65 Spanish ships survived.
8. They all survived.

Page 50

A 1. Grandpa Bob is more likely to read books.
2. Auntie Deera is most likely to enjoy food because we are told she is plump.
3. (possible answer) Auntie Deera was tall and thin with a sharp, sullen face.
4. Zak is the youngest because the text implies that he is ten years old.
5. Charlie is probably a teenager.

Page 54

A 7, 3, 1, 5, 2, 4, 6

Notes